DVD STUDY GUIDE

RICK WARREN

We Were Made for Relationships

DVD STUDY GUIDE

A SIX-SESSION VIDEO-BASED STUDY FOR SMALL GROUPS

ZONDERVAN®

ZONDERVAN.com/
AUTHORTRACKER
follow your favorite authors

ZONDERVAN

40 Days of Love DVD Study Guide
Copyright © 2009 by Rick Warren

Requests for information should be addressed to:

Zondervan, *Grand Rapids, Michigan 49530*

ISBN 978-0-310-32687-8

Cover design: *Julie Head*
Interior design: *Beth Shagene*

Printed in the United States of America

09 10 11 12 13 14 15 • 24 23 22 21 20 19 18 17 16 15 14 13 12 11 10 9 8 7 6 5 4 3 2 1

Contents

Understanding Your Study Guide

Here is a brief explanation of the features of this study guide.

- **Looking Ahead/Catching Up:** You will open each meeting with an opportunity for everyone to check in with each other about how you are doing with the weekly assignments. Accountability is a key to success in this study!

- **Key Verse:** Each week you will find a key verse or Scripture passage for your group to read together. If someone in the group has a different translation, ask them to read it aloud so the group can get a bigger picture of the meaning of the passage.

- **Video Lessons:** There is a video lesson for the group to watch together. Fill in the blanks in the lesson outlines as you watch the video, and be sure to refer back to these outlines during your discussion time.

- **Discovery Questions:** Each video segment is complemented by several questions for group discussion. Please don't feel pressured to discuss every single question. Give everyone ample opportunity to share their thoughts. If you don't get through all of the discussion questions, that's okay.

- **Living on Purpose:** In his book, *The Purpose Driven Life*, Rick Warren identifies God's five purposes for our lives. They are worship, fellowship, discipleship, ministry, and evangelism. We will focus on one of these five purposes in each lesson, and discuss how it relates to the subject of the study. This section is very important, so please be sure to leave time for it.

- **Diving Deeper:** The material in this small group study is designed to complement the book, *The Relationship Principles of Jesus*, by Tom Holladay (Zondervan, 2008). Each week, this section will direct you to readings from the book for greater understanding of the topic.

- **Prayer Direction:** At the end of each session you will find suggestions for your group prayer time. Praying together is one of the greatest privileges of small group life. Please don't take it for granted.

Your group will not just be studying love—you will be practicing love. Everyone will greatly benefit by doing the Putting It into Practice and Reaching Out Together activities.

- **Putting It into Practice:** This is where the rubber meets the road. We don't want to be just hearers of the Word. We also need to be doers of the Word (James 1:22). This section provides an opportunity for each group member to focus on one relationship each week (a "One Person Assignment"). It is introduced in more detail in Session One on page 21. Because it encourages individuals to develop or deepen relationships, it is an important part of *40 Days of Love*.

- **Reaching Out Together:** A practical action of love that your group will plan and do together for someone else. This ministry project is introduced in Session Two (page 35) and also discussed in Session Five (page 71).

- **Host Tips:** These brief instructions are helpful coaching hints for your group host. Here's your first tip:

HOST TIP

The study guide material is meant to be your servant, not your master. The point is not to race through the sessions; the point is to take time to let God work in your lives. Nor is it necessary to "go around the circle" before you move on to the next question. Give people the freedom to speak, but don't insist that they do. Your group will enjoy deeper, more open sharing and discussion if people don't feel pressured to speak up.

How to Use This Video Curriculum

Follow these four simple steps for a successful small group meeting:

1. Open your group meeting by using the Looking Ahead or Catching Up sections of your study guide.

2. Watch the video lesson together and follow along in the outlines in this study guide.

3. Complete the rest of the discussion materials for each session, including the Living on Purpose and Prayer Direction sections.

4. Review the Putting It into Practice and Diving Deeper assignments and commit to doing them before your next meeting.

READ THE BOOK!

To maximize the impact of this study, we recommend that each participant have a copy of this study guide and the book *The Relationship Principles of Jesus*, by Tom Holladay, teaching pastor at Saddleback Church. Reading assignments and in-group review of *The Relationship Principles of Jesus* are a vital part of this learning experience. The book will become a valuable, permanent resource for review and sharing once you have completed this study.

Love Matters Most

Looking Ahead

1. Welcome to *40 Days of Love*. If your group is new or if you have new members, take time to briefly introduce yourselves and to review the Group Guidelines on page 95–96.

2. Share with the group what you hope to get out of this study.

3. If you search the Internet for love songs, you will find more than thirty-nine million entries! Name some of your favorites, and discuss what they say about love.

Key Verse

Let love be your highest goal!
1 Corinthians 14:1 (NLT)

HOST TIP

The key verse establishes the theme and binds the group with the "glue" of God's Word. Have someone read the passage aloud.

Watch the Session One video now and fill in the blanks in the outline on pages 15–18. Refer back to the outline during your discussion time.

Love Matters Most

The Bible can be summarized in one word:

relationship.

Three Reasons Why Love Needs to Be Your Number One Priority

1. Love is the _____ in life.

> [37]*Jesus replied, "'You must love the LORD your God with all your heart, all your soul, and all your mind.' [38]This is the first and greatest commandment. [39]A second is equally important: 'Love your neighbor as yourself.'"* (Matthew 22:37 – 39 NLT)

Get the message: relationships — love — is what matters most in life.

> *The entire law is summed up in a single command: "Love your neighbor as yourself."* (Galatians 5:14 NIV)

Human love wears out, but God's love lasts forever.

2. Love is the _____ **of life.**

If I don't live a life of love ...

nothing I _____ will matter.

If I could speak in any language in heaven or on earth but didn't love others, I would only be making meaningless noise like a loud gong or a clanging cymbal. (1 Corinthians 13:1 NLT)

Words without love are worthless.

If I don't live a life of love ...

nothing I _____ will matter.

I may have the gift of prophecy. I may understand all the secret things of God and have all knowledge ... if I do not have love, then I am nothing. (1 Corinthians 13:2 NCV)

Brilliance without love equals zero.

If I don't live a life of love ...

nothing I _____ will matter.

Even if I had the gift of faith so that I could speak to a mountain and make it move, I would still be worth nothing at all without love. (1 Corinthians 13:2 TLB)

Faith without love does not matter.

If I don't live a life of love ...

nothing I _____ will matter.

If I gave everything I have to the poor and even sacrificed my body ... but if I didn't love others, I would be of no value whatsoever. (1 Corinthians 13:3 NLT)

Giving is not necessarily loving.

If I don't live a life of love ...

nothing I _____ will matter.

No matter what I say, what I believe, and what I do, I'm bankrupt without love. (1 Corinthians 13:3 MSG)

Relationships are more important than accomplishments.

3. Love is the _____ in life.

There are three things that will endure — faith, hope, and love — and the greatest of these is love. (1 Corinthians 13:13 NLT)

God has shown us how to leave a lasting legacy — fill your life with love.

To deepen your love:

- Commit to meet with your small group these next six weeks.

- Commit to go to church together each weekend during this study.

- Do the daily reading in *The Relationship Principles of Jesus.*

- Practice acting in unselfish and loving ways.

> *Keep company with him and learn a life of love. Observe how Christ loved us. His love was not cautious but extravagant. He didn't love in order to get something from us but to give everything of himself to us. Love like that.* (Ephesians 5:2 MSG)

Discovery Questions

1. "I love ice cream. I love my kids. I love God. I love those shoes." What does this tell us about the meaning of the word "love"?

2. Who is the most loving person you have ever known, and what did their life look like?

3. What practical advice do you think they would give about how to show love to the people in your life?

4. Pastor Rick said that if we don't live a life of love, nothing we say, know, believe, give, or accomplish will matter (see pages 16 – 17 in your outline notes). Which of the five speaks to you the most? How can you improve in that area?

Living on Purpose: Worship

Have a group member read the following passage aloud.

When asked "What is the greatest commandment?" Jesus said:

> *37"You must love the LORD your God with all your heart, all your soul, and all your mind.... 39Love your neighbor as yourself."*
> (Matthew 22:37, 39 NLT)

What does it look like to love God with your whole being?

Sometimes the second part (love your neighbor) is more difficult than the first part (love God with all you've got). How can loving others be an act of worship?

Putting It into Practice:
The One Person Assignment

How does a person go from talking about love to living a life of love? This One Person Assignment exercise will give you an opportunity to show love to at least one person each week. Take time as a group to read and discuss these guidelines, then follow the suggested action for this session.

One Person Assignment Guidelines

Turn talk into action by reaching out to one person in a loving, unselfish way this week.

1. You can pick the same person or a different person each week.

2. It can be a close relationship or a distant one. The relationship doesn't have to be one in crisis — it can be a good relationship you want to improve.

3. The individual you choose can be:
   - a person in your group
   - a family member
   - your spouse
   - a person who needs the Lord
   - your neighbor
   - someone you work with
   - a person on the fringes of your life or church
   - a lonely person
   - anyone the Lord puts on your heart

4. Each week you will receive a suggestion on how to reach out to the person you have chosen. You may want to write down the person's name next to the key verse in the Small Group Resources section (page 110). Pray for that person at least once next week and make a connection to develop or deepen your relationship.

Action for Session One

Think of someone you haven't shown love to recently — a friend, family member, colleague, etc. In what way can you apply this week's lesson to that relationship?

Here are some ideas to get you started:

- Take them out for coffee.

- Send a note, card, or email.

- Give them a call to see how they're doing.

- Ask how you can pray for them.

- Invite them to join your group.

Choose a practical action step and tell your group what you are going to do.

Diving Deeper

How do we bridge the relationship gap — the gap between what we hope for in a relationship and what we actually experience? Begin to explore this issue by reading chapters 1 – 7 in *The Relationship Principles of Jesus*. Be prepared to share your thoughts and insights with the group next week.

Prayer Direction

1. We love God because he first loved us. Think about a time when the Lord showed you that he loved you. Take a few moments to voice thanks to God for loving you at that point in your life.

2. Ask the Lord to help you choose love. Use this concluding prayer as a guide:

   "Thank you, God, for loving me in spite of my imperfections. I have to admit that as hard as I try, I have difficulty loving some people. Help me trust you for the power to love. Lord, I turn to you for wisdom as I focus on one person to love this week. Help me to show that I love you by loving others. In Jesus' name, amen."

NOTES

Love Is Patient,
Love Is Kind

Catching Up

1. As you read *The Relationship Principles of Jesus* this past week, you focused on how you spend your time, money, and resources. What did it say to you about the top priorities in your life?

2. In your Putting It into Practice exercise from the last session, you were encouraged to reach out in a loving way to someone. How did it go? Share your experience.

Key Verse

Love is patient, love is kind.
1 Corinthians 13:4 (NIV)

Watch the Session Two video now and fill in the blanks in the outline on pages 27 – 32. Refer back to the outline during your discussion time.

Love Is Patient,
Love Is Kind

The Secret to Patience

You _____ with God.

- God's part is to provide the _____.

- Your part is to provide the _____.

> ³We can rejoice, too, when we run into problems and trials
> for we know that they are good for us — they help us learn
> to be patient. ⁴And patience develops strength of character
> in us and helps us trust God more each time we use it
> until finally our hope and faith are strong and steady.
> (Romans 5:3–4 TLB)

THREE THINGS WILL HELP YOU
RESPOND WITH PATIENCE

1. Discover a _____.

> *A man's wisdom gives him patience; it is to his glory to overlook an offense.* (Proverbs 19:11 NIV)

2. Deepen _____.

When you're filled with love, almost nothing will irritate you. But when you're filled with anger, almost anything will irritate you.

3. Depend on _____.

> *We also pray that you will be strengthened with all his glorious power so you will have all the endurance and patience you need. May you be filled with joy.* (Colossians 1:11 NLT)

The Secret to Kindness

Kindness is _____.

FOUR LESSONS FROM THE GOOD SAMARITAN
(Luke 10:30 – 35)

1. Start _____ of people around us.

Kindness begins with the eyes.

> *When he saw the man's condition, his heart went out to him.*
> (Luke 10:33 MSG)

Why don't we see the wounds of the people around us?

_____.

To be a kinder person, you must slow down.

> *Look out for the good of others also.* (1 Corinthians 10:24 NCV)

RATE YOURSELF: Do I see the needs of others? (Sensitivity)

1	2	3	4	5
I really need to work on this	Rarely	Sometimes	Often	Everything is great

2. _____ with people's pain.

When he saw him, his heart was filled with pity. (Luke 10:33 TEV)

Weep with those who weep. (Romans 12:15 TEV)

Sympathy begins with the ears.

Share each other's troubles and problems, and in this way obey the law of Christ. (Galatians 6:2 NLT)

RATE YOURSELF: Do I listen to the needs of others? (Sympathy)

1	2	3	4	5
No, I don't pay attention at all	Rarely	Sometimes	Often	Yes, I'm a good listener

3. _____.

Kneeling beside him the Samaritan soothed his wounds with medicine and bandaged them. (Luke 10:34 TLB)

The Good Samaritan did three things:

• He stooped down and got on the man's level.
• He used what he had (wine and oil).
• He dressed him with bandages (he tore up his own clothes).

The Good Samaritan did what he could with what he had at that particular moment.

Never walk away from someone who deserves help; your hand is God's hand for that person. (Proverbs 3:27 MSG)

Never tell your neighbors to wait until tomorrow if you can help them now. (Proverbs 3:28 TEV)

To be a kinder person like the Good Samaritan:

• You must be willing to be _____.

• You must be willing to _____.

> *There is no fear in love; but perfect love casts out fear.* (1 John 4:18 NASB)

RATE YOURSELF: How quickly do I respond to a need when I see it? (Spontaneous Kindness)

1	2	3	4	5
I intend to do it but don't	Rarely	Sometimes	Often	I act immediately

4. _____ whatever it takes.

There is always a cost to kindness.

> *³⁴"Then he put the man on his own donkey and took him to an inn, where he took care of him. ³⁵The next day he handed the innkeeper two silver coins, telling him, 'Take care of this man. If his bill runs higher than this, I'll pay you the next time I'm here.'"* (Luke 10:34–35 NLT)

Kindness is doing something for somebody without expecting anything in return.

> *⁷Share your food with the hungry and bring poor, homeless people into your own homes.... ⁸Then your light will shine like the dawn.... ¹¹The LORD will always lead you. He will satisfy your needs in dry lands.... You will be like a garden that has much water, like a spring that never runs dry.* (Isaiah 58:7, 8, 11 NCV)

> *The LORD is merciful! He is kind and patient, and his love never fails.* (Psalm 103:8 CEV)

Discovery Questions

1. Have you ever needed a "Good Samaritan" when you were hurting? Did anyone ignore your need and pass you by? What help did you receive?

2. Which was the greater risk for the Samaritan—helping in the immediate crisis, or coming back to follow up in a longer-term commitment? Why?

3. Pastor Rick compared our lives to a full cup. If a cup filled with coffee is jiggled, coffee spills out. What spills out of your life when you are "jiggled"?

Are you filled with patience or impatience? Kindness or indifference? What do your reactions to difficult people and situations reveal about the content of your character cup?

4. What can you do to make sure you are filled with the right stuff?

Living on Purpose: Ministry

It would have been easier for the Samaritan if he had not been alone as he helped the injured man.

What can your group do together to express love to a hurting person outside your group? Have someone read the Reaching Out Together instructions that follow. Begin to discuss ideas for a group ministry project.

Reaching Out Together

Reaching Out Together is a practical action of love your group will do for someone.

1. Plan an event when your group can reach out to a person in your church, community, or beyond.

2. Do something practical. It doesn't have to be big to be significant.

3. Ask God to show you what he would have you do. Some ideas to get you started:
   - Babysit for a single parent in your neighborhood.
   - Bring a meal to a family in need.
   - Offer to mow a neighbor's yard.
   - Have all the families in your group collect their giveaway clothes together and take them to a shelter or organization in your community.
   - Find someone in your community who is facing tough times and visit them and pray with them as a group.
   - Volunteer to tutor kids at your neighborhood school.
   - Prepare a welcome basket for someone new in your community. Drop it off and get to know them.

Continued on next page.

- Pinpoint a house in your neighborhood that needs some help. Reach out to the family and offer to paint a fence, fix the porch, etc. (Keep it small but heartfelt.)
- Offer to help in the public library reading to kids.
- Offer to clean up a local beach.
- Volunteer at a homeless shelter in your community.

4. Aim to begin the Reaching Out Together project by your last session.

Putting It into Practice:
The One Person Assignment

This coming week, look for a person who needs your kindness or patience. That individual may be injured emotionally, spiritually, relationally, physically, or financially. Who do you know that needs a "Good Samaritan" in their life right now? What do you have to give? Rather than passing by, reach out to the person this week and do a specific act of kindness. "Your hand is God's hand for that person" (Proverbs 3:27 MSG).

Diving Deeper

For a better understanding of how to love like Jesus loves, read chapters 8 – 14 in *The Relationship Principles of Jesus* this week.

Author Tom Holladay writes:

> Relationships are like competing in the Indy 500. We're not talking about a lazy trip down some quiet country road. Relationships are complicated, high-speed stuff.... To be successful in the Indy 500, you need a professional driver. When it comes to relationships, there's only one professional who drove this course—Jesus. He's the one who made relationships, and he's the one who can empower them and steer them in the right direction.

Prayer Direction

1. Pastor Rick asked you to rate yourself in three areas: sensitivity, sympathy, and spontaneous kindness. Which area challenges you the most? In silent prayer, ask God for his power to help you improve in that area. Allow several minutes for everybody to finish praying.

2. Close in prayer, asking the Lord to help you see and hear the needs of others and to be willing to be interrupted by them. Ask God to empower everyone to reach out to another person with patience or kindness next week. Ask for God's leading as you choose your Reaching Out Together group ministry project.

NOTES

Love Speaks
the Truth

Catching Up

1. Did you read chapters 8 – 14 in *The Relationship Principles of Jesus*? Share something you read that was particularly meaningful to you.

2. When it comes to conflict, are you a turtle or a skunk? A turtle hides its head at the first sign of trouble. A skunk lets everybody know how it feels.

Key Verse

Love ... rejoices with the truth.

1 Corinthians 13:6 (NIV)

Watch the Session Three video now and fill in the blanks in the outline on pages 42 – 44. Refer back to the outline during your discussion time.

Love Speaks
the Truth

Most people misunderstand the phrase "keeping the peace," and think it means avoiding confrontation at all costs. But repressing the truth rather than dealing with the truth causes trouble.

Someone who holds back the truth causes trouble, but the one who openly [confronts] works for peace. (Proverbs 10:10 TEV)

Speak … the truth in a spirit of love. (Ephesians 4:15 TEV)

How to Speak the Truth in Love

1. Check your _____.

What is the right motive? _____

_____.

> We tell you this as Christ's servants.... Everything we do, dear
> friends, is for your benefit. (2 Corinthians 12:19 NLT)

To go from shallow to intimate relationships, you need to go
through the "tunnel of truth" where you deal with issues you
really don't want to deal with.

2. Plan your _____.

> Intelligent people think before they speak; what they say is then
> more persuasive. (Proverbs 16:23 TEV)

> For I wrote you out of great distress and anguish of heart and
> with many tears, not to grieve you but to let you know the depth
> of my love for you. (2 Corinthians 2:4 NIV)

Keys to Presenting the Truth in Love

1. Plan _____ you're going to say it.

| **Don't** say it when the person is:
• tired
• under pressure
• in a hurry | **Do** say it when …
• it is the best timing for the person
• the person is rested and ready to hear it
• you both are at your best
• you have privacy |

2. Plan _____ you're going to say.

   The right word at the right time is like precious gold set in silver. (Proverbs 25:11 CEV)

   a. **Introduction:** How you introduce a touchy subject will determine whether it's going to be received well or rejected.

| **Don't** start with sarcasm or anger. | **Do** start with humility and gentleness. |

   b. **Illustrations:** Help the person picture what you want to say.

| **Don't** just choose illustrations you like. | **Do** choose illustrations the person understands. |

3. Plan _____ you're going to say it.

   Thoughtless words can wound as deeply as any sword, but wisely spoken words can heal. (Proverbs 12:18 TEV)
   A soft answer turns away wrath. (Proverbs 15:1 NKJV)

| **Don't …**
• say it thoughtlessly, or it will hurt the person
• say it offensively, or it will be received defensively | **Do …**
• lower your voice
• say it in a gentle and humble way |

Truth + Tact + Timing = _____

3. Give them _____.

A word of encouragement does wonders! (Proverbs 12:25 TLB)

Affirm that:

- You deeply love and care for the person.
- You will pray for them and help them.
- You believe they can change.
- The relationship can be better and that you can be even closer as a result of this confrontation.

4. Risk their _____.

The apostle Paul risked rejection and it turned out well:

⁷"I know I distressed you greatly with my letter. Although I felt awful at the time, I don't feel at all bad now that I see how it turned out. The letter upset you, but only for a while.... ⁹You were jarred into turning things around. You let the distress bring you to God.... ¹²And that is what I was hoping for in the first place when I wrote the letter." (2 Corinthians 7:8 - 9, 12 MSG)

Discovery Questions

1. We wouldn't let a friend step into oncoming traffic. Why then do we hesitate to stop a friend who is stepping into trouble or making a harmful choice?

2. The right reason for confronting a person in love is to help, not to hurt. If you sense your motive to speak the truth in love is not pure, what needs to change in you? What should you do?

3. Describe a time when someone was honest and loving enough to tell you what you needed to hear, rather than just what you wanted to hear. How did it help you?

4. Are you willing to hear the truth in love? What can you do to prepare your heart to hear it?

Living on Purpose:
Fellowship and Evangelism

HOST TIP

You may choose one or both purposes, depending on the group's composition.

Honest communication impacts people in big ways. Pastor Rick said, "Imagine what would happen if all those under-the-surface tensions were dissipated—in our church, in our small groups, at the workplace, in our marriages—because we cared enough to speak the truth in love."

One of you read this passage aloud:

> *[19]My dear friends, if you know people who have wandered off from God's truth, don't write them off. Go after them. Get them back [20]and you will have rescued precious lives from destruction and prevented an epidemic of wandering away from God.* (James 5:19-20 MSG)

Fellowship

If you speak the truth in love to a fellow believer on an unhealthy path, what would be the impact on the body of Christ if the person changes direction?

Evangelism

How can speaking the truth in love open the door to sharing your faith with an unbeliever?

Putting It into Practice:
The One Person Assignment

Confronting in love is not just a one-time action; it takes time to plan. In the first discovery question, we said that we would prevent a friend from stepping out in traffic. This person also might be going the wrong direction in another part of their life. Has God laid someone on your heart — a young person, neighbor, friend, or family member — that you might be able to help set on the right path? Go through this exercise with that person in mind.

1. **Choose the person:** Ask yourself, "Who in my life needs to hear affirming truth?" Or ask, "Who do I need to have an honest conversation with, and can I risk approaching them?"

2. **Affirm the person:** Make a list of the positive qualities of the person you feel God is laying on your heart.

3. **Plan your presentation:** Turn to Pastor Rick's instructions on page 43. Read over the three main points—plan when you'll say it, what you'll say, and how you'll say it. Use this section later as a checklist.

   Are you planning to approach an unbeliever? Instead of just saying, "I don't like what you are doing," find a way to bring the grace, mercy, and love of Jesus into the conversation.

4. **Prepare your heart:** Check your motives. Ensure that they are aligned with God's loving heart.

5. **Forgive:** Have you forgiven the person you are thinking of confronting? Next week your group will discuss forgiveness. If you are holding onto unforgiveness, allow your heart time to go through a healing and forgiveness process before you confront anybody.

6. **Get support:** Have a conversation (not a gossip session) with a trusted friend or a group member to discuss your plan. You will need someone praying with you and for you in this process.

Diving Deeper

Read about the connection between your heart and how you communicate in chapters 15–21 of *The Relationship Principles of Jesus.*

Prayer Direction

1. Jesus taught us to take the log out of our own eye before we take the speck out of our brother's eye (Matthew 7:5). Take time to search your heart, asking the Lord to help you hear the truth in love for your own life. Pray that your heart would be open and humble before him.

2. If God has laid someone on your heart who needs to hear the truth in love, join with two or three other prayer partners in your group right now. Without going into specific details, pray for God's direction and timing on when you should initiate the conversation. Ask God to give you favor with that person, and to give you the ability, wisdom, and courage to speak with genuine love and honesty.

NOTES

SESSION FOUR

Love Is Forgiving

Catching Up

1. You're at the halfway point of this study! How is your perspective of love changing? Take a few moments to share.

2. Share an insight from your reading in chapters 15–21 in *The Relationship Principles of Jesus.*

3. In the last session, we talked about speaking the truth in love. Would anyone like to talk about a tough conversation you had this week in which you applied the lessons you learned?

Key Verse

*Love ... doesn't keep a record
of wrongs that others do.*
1 Corinthians 13:5 (CEV)

Watch the Session Four video now and fill in the blanks in the outline on pages 56 - 58. Refer back to the outline during your discussion time.

Love Is Forgiving

A Test of Love

The ultimate test of love is how you respond when somebody hurts you.

Forgiveness Quiz

T   F   A person should not be forgiven until they ask for it.

T   F   Forgiveness includes minimizing the offense and the pain that was caused.

T   F   Forgiveness includes restoring trust and reuniting a relationship.

T   F   You haven't really forgiven others until you have forgotten the offense.

---

1. Forgiveness is not _____

_____ of the offense.

Being wounded and being wronged are two different things:

- Being wounded is accidental.
- Being wronged is intentional.

2. Forgiveness is not _____

_____ without changes.

- Forgiveness is instant, but trust must be built over a long period of time.
- Forgiveness takes care of the damage done by "letting the person off the hook," but does not guarantee the relationship will be restored.

To restore a relationship, the offender must:

- demonstrate _____.

- _____ wherever

   possible.

- _____ over time.

If a person repeatedly wrongs you, you are obligated by God to forgive that person. But you are not obligated to trust that person, to let them continue to hurt you, or to instantly restore the relationship.

Three Steps of Forgiveness

1. I relinquish my _____.

> Never avenge yourselves. Leave that to God, for he has said
> that he will repay those who deserve it. (Romans 12:19 TLB)

You don't hurt the other person with your resentment — you're
only hurting yourself.

Three reasons to forgive others:

• God has _____.

• Bitterness makes you _____.

• You are going to need _____ in

 the future.

The Lord's Prayer says,

> "Forgive us our debts, as we forgive our debtors." (Matthew 6:12
> NKJV)

2. I respond to evil _____.

> 27"Do good to those who hate you, 28bless those who curse you,
> pray for those who mistreat you." (Luke 6:27-28 NIV)

> Do not be overcome by evil, but overcome evil with good.
> (Romans 12:21 NIV)

3. I _____ as long as necessary.

> [21]"Lord, how often should I forgive someone who sins against me? Seven times?" [22]"No, not seven times," Jesus replied, "but seventy times seven!" (Matthew 18:21–22 NLT)

> Remember, the Lord forgave you, so you must forgive others. (Colossians 3:13 NLT)

Don't try to forgive on your own power. Recognize and accept God's forgiveness of you. Then ask for his strength and power to go through you to forgive others.

Discovery Questions

1. Turn to the true/false quiz on page 55. Were you surprised that all of the answers were false? Which "false" seemed to be most "true" for you? Why?

2. Share a story of forgiveness you have witnessed, or share a story of how a person responded to evil with good. What did that mean to you? How did it make you feel?

3. Focus on the why of the next question—not who offended you or the details of what they did: Why is it so hard to forgive people who have hurt you? How will it affect you if you don't forgive? How will it affect you if you do forgive?

Living on Purpose:
Fellowship and Evangelism

Fellowship

1. What would happen to the relational life of the church if we would pray for those who hurt us, show patience toward those who offend us, refuse to gossip, and offer forgiveness?

2. How can your group help you deal with an area of unforgiveness in your life?

3. How can you encourage others in your group or in your church to forgive?

Evangelism

If a Christian has a strained relationship with an unbeliever (no matter who is at fault), how could experiencing forgiveness affect the unbeliever's openness to Jesus Christ?

Putting It into Practice:
The One Person Assignment

Forgiveness is often a two-way street—we need to ask for and offer it. The following questions can be hard to ask, but they are critical to your spiritual and emotional health. Right now, ask yourself, "Who do I need to ask to forgive me?" "Who do I need to forgive?"

The First Step

Pinpoint the forgiveness issue. Do you feel anxiety, anger, or other negative emotions toward anyone? Could this be a cue that you need to release that person and work on forgiveness issues in your own life?

If you are struggling with anger or bitterness toward a person, turn to Releasing Anger and Bitterness on page 103. There you will find Scriptures to help you let it go. Pick one or two verses and apply them to your situation. Allow the power of God's Word to help you release the bitterness.

The Next Step

Turn to God in prayer about this person. If you've prayed about it before and it's still bothering you, don't give up. You may use the following prayer as a model, inserting the person's name:

> Dear Lord, I may not forget, but I'm choosing to forgive
> _____. I realize trust may take time to rebuild,
> but I choose to hold no grudges. Help me to let go of bitterness
> or anger in my heart. Give me your grace that I may relinquish
> my "right" to get even. Help me understand that you have

forgiven me and that I can forgive _____ through you. I trust in your power to do that. Now, Lord, I ask you to bless _____. In particular, I ask you to bless them with these things: _____. God, please replace my hurt with your healing. Replace my pain with your peace. Replace my loss with your love. May the past truly be past. In Jesus' name I pray, amen.

The Repeated Steps

If the memory comes back and you struggle with unforgiveness again, repeat this prayer as often as you need to. Trust God in his power to help you daily. Reach out to a trusted friend or a group member to support you through this process.

Diving Deeper

In your reading this week, Tom Holladay says, "The strength to forgive someone else can only be found in the truth that you have been forgiven by God." Read chapters 22–28 in *The Relationship Principles of Jesus* and be prepared to share an insight with the group next week.

Prayer Direction

1. People who have trouble forgiving others often have trouble forgiving themselves. Have you accepted God's forgiveness? Have you forgiven yourself? In the group setting, ask God to help those of you who wrestle with these issues.

2. If group members feel comfortable doing so, pair up and pray for each other. Ask the Lord to enable your spiritual partner to give and receive forgiveness. Pray for each other that the Lord would remove any barriers to forgiveness.

3. Close with praise and thanksgiving for God's gift of forgiveness to you.

NOTES

Love Is Not Selfish

Catching Up

1. What is your most selfish hour of the week? (Your answer can be serious or silly.) What happens when someone interrupts that time?

2. Share something you read in chapters 22–28 in *The Relationship Principles of Jesus* that was particularly meaningful or challenging to you.

Key Verse

Love isn't selfish.
1 Corinthians 13:5 (CEV)

Watch the Session Five video now and fill in the blanks in the outline on pages 67–68. Refer back to the outline during your discussion time.

Love Is Not Selfish

We are a "self" conscious society.

> They all turn to their own way, each seeks his own gain. (Isaiah 56:11 NIV)

You can't be selfish and loving at the same time.

> Selfishness only causes trouble. (Proverbs 28:25 TEV)

Antidotes to Selfishness

1. Build _trust/bonds_ "deeper relationships"

> You are members of God's very own family ... and you belong in God's household with every other Christian. (Ephesians 2:19 TLB)

> Let us not give up the habit of meeting together.... Instead, let us encourage one another. (Hebrews 10:25 TEV)

2. Give _yourself away — service_

> [God has] given us new lives from Christ Jesus; and long ages ago he planned that we should spend these lives in helping others. (Ephesians 2:10 TLB)

> "Only those who throw away their lives for my sake and for the sake of the Good News will ever know what it means to really live." (Mark 8:35 TLB)

Mine all you can

3. Practice _Self Denial_.

> ⁴Look out for one another's interests, not just for your own.
> ⁵The attitude you should have is the one that Christ Jesus had.
> (Philippians 2:4 – 5 TEV)

> "If anyone would come after me, he must deny himself and take
> up his cross daily and follow me." (Luke 9:23 NIV)

On the list on page 69, put a check beside the areas where God is challenging you to grow.

Go for significance/not success

Service ⟶ Success

Denying Yourself Is When ...

☐ You can watch other people prosper and succeed without feeling jealous, but rather rejoice in their success.

☐ You see other people's needs being met with abundance, while your needs are far greater, yet you don't question God or fail to be grateful for what you do have.

☐ You choose to serve someone else and you choose to put their needs ahead of yours.

☐ You share your faith knowing that you may be insulted or put down.

☐ You don't seek praise or fish for compliments. You don't seek the approval of others. You can live without constantly being recognized and applauded.

☐ You draw out the other person in conversation instead of telling your stories and opinions.

☐ You can accept criticism willingly and learn from it with a teachable attitude.

☐ You can be content with less than the best of circumstances without griping or complaining.

☐ You accept interruptions that God places in your schedule and you patiently endure irritations.

Discovery Questions

1. When do you feel the most self-centered? Why is that?

2. Turn to the checklist on page 69 of your outline notes. Which example is the most challenging to you? Why? How will growth in this area affect your relationships?

3. How is selfishness the enemy of strong relationships?

4. Tell about a time when someone did something unselfish for you. How did it impact you?

Living on Purpose: Ministry

When you serve together, you make a difference in the lives of others, and you build strong relationships in your group.

Take time now to finish planning your group's *40 Days of Love* ministry project, Reaching Out Together. For a list of suggestions and guidelines to get you started, turn to Session Two, page 35. Then, use the checklist below:

☐ What are we going to do?

☐ Where?

☐ When (date and time)?

☐ Who will do what?

☐ What materials do we need (paint, cleaning supplies, etc.)?

Putting It into Practice:
The One Person Assignment

Philippians 2:4 says, "Look out for one another's interests" (TEV). This week, look for a person who is on the "fringes" of your life. It could be someone you don't know, or a casual acquaintance from your church, work, school, or neighborhood.

How can you refocus your attention to really see that person? Think of an unselfish act of kindness you can do for them. Do it out of conviction, not your convenience. Give without expecting anything back. Take action this week.

Diving Deeper

Let's say you are angry with a coworker, and out of frustration you feel like bending all his paper clips into pretzel shapes. How can you straighten out your attitude toward this person and relate to him kindly? Read chapters 29–35 in *The Relationship Principles of Jesus*. Be prepared to share an insight you gained in your next session.

Prayer Direction

Choose one for your group:

1. Pray together for your group ministry project. Ask for changed lives, both inside and outside the group. Pray that your group would bind together in loving ways, and that people will be touched by God's love through you. If you have completed your project, pray for the people you have already touched.

2. Break up into groups of three or four. Pray for one another to overcome shyness, busyness, selfishness, or anything that may hinder your ability to reach out to others.

3. Ask the Lord to help each of you be more sensitive to the needs of a specific person outside of your normal circle of friends and family. Pray for the Lord to help you serve that person, even though they may not return the favor. Conclude by thanking the Lord for showing you how to really live.

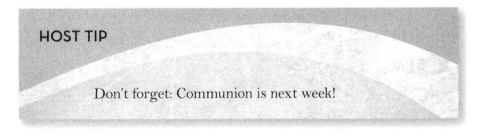

HOST TIP

Don't forget: Communion is next week!

NOTES

The Habits
of a Loving Heart

Catching Up

1. When you feel tired or depleted, how do you recharge?

2. Has your group completed your Reaching Out Together project?
   If so, what did you learn from your experience? If not, what do
   you hope to learn?

3. Share a meaningful "nugget" you discovered this past week in *The
   Relationship Principles of Jesus.*

Key Verse

[Love] always protects, always trusts,
always hopes, always perseveres.
1 Corinthians 13:7 (NIV)

Watch the Session Six video now and fill in the
blanks in the outline on pages 77–79. Refer back
to the outline during your discussion time.

The Habits
of a Loving Heart

*[Love] always protects, always trusts, always hopes, always
perseveres.* (1 Corinthians 13:7 NIV)

"I have loved you with an everlasting love." (Jeremiah 31:3 NIV)

*Love knows no limit to its endurance, no end to its trust, no
fading of its hope; it can outlast anything.* (1 Corinthians 13:7 PH)

1. Develop habits that refresh me _____.

Three physical habits of a loving heart:

● _____

*It is senseless for you to work so hard from early morning until
late at night ... God wants his loved ones to get their proper
rest.* (Psalm 127:2 TLB)

● _____

You made my body, Lord; now give me sense to heed your laws.
(Psalm 119:73 TLB)

● _____

Honor God with your body. (1 Corinthians 6:20 NLT)

2. Develop habits that recharge me _____.

Three emotional habits of a loving heart:

• _____

   So many people were coming and going … [Jesus] said to them, "Come with me by yourselves to a quiet place and get some rest." (Mark 6:31 NIV)

• _____

   [Jesus] came, enjoying life … (Luke 7:34 PH)

• _____

   Being cheerful keeps you healthy. (Proverbs 17:22 TEV)

3. Develop habits that renew me _____.

   Take time and trouble to keep yourself spiritually fit. (1 Timothy 4:7 PH)

Three spiritual habits of a loving heart:

• _____

The outward man does indeed suffer wear and tear, but every day the inward man receives fresh strength. (2 Corinthians 4:16 PH)

Rick Warren's Bible Study Methods available at SaddlebackResources.com

RICK WARREN'S BIBLE STUDY METHODS

- _____

Two are stronger than one. (Ecclesiastes 4:9)

- _____

I will sing of your strength, in the morning I will sing of your love; for you are my ... refuge in times of trouble. (Psalm 59:16 NIV)

"Come to me, all of you who are weary and carry heavy burdens, and I will give you rest." (Matthew 11:28 NLT)

The quality of your relationship to God determines the quality of every other relationship you have.

Did you pray with Pastor Rick and open your life to Jesus Christ for the first time? Speak to your host or one of the group members now or after the meeting and tell them of your decision.

Other Resources Mentioned by Pastor Rick

- Tell your story or write about your group and send it to *PastorRick@saddleback.com.*
- Sign up for Pastor Rick's free daily devotional at *PurposeDrivenLife.com.*
- Find other small group resources at *SaddlebackResources.com.*

Discovery Questions

1. Which habit of a loving heart do you need to work on the most — physical, emotional, or spiritual? How would strengthening that habit help your love to last?

2. What is something practical you can do to develop that habit? Share thoughts and practical tips with the group.

3. What is the greatest lesson you have learned about love in the last six weeks? How has it impacted your relationships?

4. How has this study helped you to rely on Christ's strength to love others?

Living on Purpose:
Discipleship and Fellowship

Discipleship

> *Let us think of ways to motivate one another to acts of love and good works.* (Hebrews 10:24 NLT)

Turn to your notes on pages 77–79, together. Under each main category (physical, emotional, and spiritual habits) are three things you can do to strengthen each habit. If you have not already done so, select the habit you need or want to work on.

Choose someone in your group to be your spiritual partner in the following exercise. If possible, choose someone who is strong in your area of weakness.

Discuss with each other the area you chose. Offer insight to motivate your partner to develop the habit they selected, and have them do the same for you. Write down at least one action step you will take this week. During Prayer Direction you will pray for one another.

Fellowship

The Lord's Supper offers us a chance to quietly explore the depth of Jesus' love for us, but there is more to it than that. Following that first Communion, Jesus gave us a new commandment: love one another. When we celebrate the Lord's Supper, it is a statement of our love for the Lord, but it is also a statement of our love for each other. Communion is meant to be shared in community.

Turn to page 106 for guidelines for serving the Lord's Supper.

Putting It into Practice

Pass it on — that is the whole point of this study!

Who do you know that will benefit by reading *The Relationship Principles of Jesus?* You can lend them your book or buy them a copy of their own. You might even consider starting another *40 Days of Love* study with a different group of people to share what you have learned.

However God leads you, this is too good to keep to yourself. News about real love is good news. Pass it on. You will be blessed, and so will someone else.

Diving Deeper

The goal of love is not some false ideal; rather it is seeing God at work in our real lives: "Forget the ideal, and go for the real!" Finish reading chapters 36–40 in *The Relationship Principles of Jesus* this week.

Prayer Direction

1. Turn to your spiritual partner again and pray about the specific habits you have each chosen to work on. Pray that God would show you both how to grow in the practice of that habit.

2. Come together as a group. Agree in prayer to ask for Christ's strength and empowerment to love. Give time for individuals to express thanksgiving for what he has done in their lives through *40 Days of Love*.

What Next?

1. If you enjoyed *40 Days of Love*, discuss what study your group would like to do next.

2. The resources Pastor Rick mentioned are listed at the end of your outline notes on page 79.

3. Stay in touch with group members. Phone, email, meet for coffee — get creative as you ask one another, "How are you doing?"

NOTES

Small Group Resources

Helps for Hosts

Top Ten Ideas for New Hosts

Congratulations! As the host of your small group, you have responded to the call to help shepherd Jesus' flock. Few other tasks in the family of God surpass the contribution you will be making. As you prepare to facilitate your group, whether it is one session or the entire series, here are a few thoughts to keep in mind.

Remember you are not alone. God knows everything about you, and he knew you would be asked to facilitate your group. Even though you may not feel ready, this is common for all good hosts. God promises, "I will never leave you; I will never abandon you" (Hebrews 13:5 TEV). Whether you are facilitating for one evening, several weeks, or a lifetime, you will be blessed as you serve.

1. **Don't try to do it alone.** Pray right now for God to help you build a healthy team. If you can enlist a cohost to help you shepherd the group, you will find your experience much richer. This is your chance to involve as many people as you can in building a healthy group. All you have to do is ask people to help. You'll be surprised at the response.

2. **Be friendly and be yourself.** God wants to use your unique gifts and temperament. Be sure to greet people at the door with a big smile. This can set the mood for the whole gathering. Remember, they are taking as big a step to show up at your house as you are to host this group! Don't try to do things exactly like another host; do them in a way that fits you. Admit when you don't have an answer and apologize when you make a mistake. Your group will love you for it and you'll sleep better at night.

3. **Prepare for your meeting ahead of time.** Watch the "Helps for Hosts" video segment before each lesson, then review the session and write down your responses to each question. Pay special attention to exercises that ask group members to do something other than engage in discussion. These exercises will help your group live what the Bible teaches, not just talk about it. Be sure you understand how an exercise works. If the exercise employs one of the items in the Group Resources section (such as the Group Guidelines), be sure to look over that item so you'll know how it works.

4. **Pray for your group members by name.** Before your group arrives, take a few moments and pray for each member by name. You may want to review the prayer list at least once a week. Ask God to use your time together to touch the heart of every person in your group. Expect God to lead you to whomever he wants you to encourage or challenge in a special way. If you listen, God will surely lead.

5. **When you ask a question, be patient.** Someone will eventually respond. Sometimes people need a moment or two of silence to think about the question. If silence doesn't bother you, it won't bother anyone else. After someone responds, affirm the response with a simple "thanks" or "great answer." Then ask, "How about somebody else?" or "Would someone who hasn't shared like to add anything?" Be sensitive to new people or reluctant members who aren't ready to say, pray, or do anything. If you give them a safe setting, they will blossom over time. If someone in your group is a wallflower who sits silently through every session, consider talking to them privately and encouraging them to participate. Let them know how important they are to you—that they are loved and appreciated—and that the group would value their input. Remember, still water often runs deep.

6. **Provide transitions between questions.** Ask if anyone would like to read the paragraph or Bible passage. Don't call on anyone, but ask for a volunteer, and then be patient until someone begins. Be sure to thank the person who reads aloud.

7. **Break into smaller groups occasionally.** With a greater opportunity to talk in a small circle, people will connect more with the study, apply more quickly what they're learning, and ultimately get more out of their small group experience. A small circle also encourages a quiet person to participate and tends to minimize the effects of a more vocal or dominant member.

8. **Small circles are also helpful during prayer time.** People who are unaccustomed to praying aloud will feel more comfortable trying it with just two or three others. Also, prayer requests won't take as much time, so circles will have more time to actually pray. When you gather back with the whole group, you can have one person from each circle briefly update everyone on the prayer requests from their subgroups. The other great aspect of subgrouping is that it fosters leadership development. As you ask people in the group to facilitate discussion or lead a prayer circle, it gives them a small leadership step that can build their confidence.

9. **Rotate facilitators occasionally.** You may be perfectly capable of hosting each time, but you will help others grow in their faith and gifts if you give them opportunities to host the group.

10. **One final challenge (for new or first-time hosts).** Before your first opportunity to lead, look up each of the six passages that follow. Read each one as a devotional exercise to help prepare you with a shepherd's heart. Trust us on this one.

If you do this, you will be more than ready for your first meeting.

Matthew 9:36 – 38 (NIV)

36When [Jesus] saw the crowds, he had compassion on them, because they were harassed and helpless, like sheep without a shepherd. 37Then he said to his disciples, "The harvest is plentiful but the workers are few. 38Ask the Lord of the harvest, therefore, to send out workers into his harvest field."

John 10:14 – 15 (NIV)

14"I am the good shepherd; I know my sheep and my sheep know me — 15just as the Father knows me and I know the Father — and I lay down my life for the sheep."

1 Peter 5:2 – 4 (NIV)

2Be shepherds of God's flock that is under your care, serving as overseers — not because you must, but because you are willing, as God wants you to be; 3not greedy for money, but eager to serve; not lording it over those entrusted to you, but being examples to the flock. 4And when the Chief Shepherd appears, you will receive the crown of glory that will never fade away.

Philippians 2:1 – 5 (NIV)

1If you have any encouragement from being united with Christ, if any comfort from his love, if any fellowship with the Spirit, if any tenderness and compassion, 2then make my joy complete by being like-minded, having the same love, being one in spirit and purpose. 3Do nothing out of selfish ambition or vain conceit, but in humility consider others better than yourselves. 4Each of you should look not only to your own interests, but also to the interests of others. 5Your attitude should be the same as that of Jesus Christ.

Hebrews 10:23-25 (NIV)

²³Let us hold unswervingly to the hope we profess, for he who promised is faithful. ²⁴And let us consider how we may spur one another on toward love and good deeds. ²⁵Let us not give up meeting together, as some are in the habit of doing, but let us encourage one another — and all the more as you see the Day approaching.

1 Thessalonians 2:7-8, 11-12 (NIV)

⁷ ... but we were gentle among you, like a mother caring for her little children. ⁸We loved you so much that we were delighted to share with you not only the gospel of God but our lives as well, because you had become so dear to us. ¹¹For you know that we dealt with each of you as a father deals with his own children, ¹²encouraging, comforting and urging you to live lives worthy of God, who calls you into his kingdom and glory.

Frequently Asked Questions

How long will this group meet?

40 Days of Love is six sessions long. We encourage your group to add a seventh session for a celebration. In your final session, each group member may decide if he or she desires to continue on for another study. At that time you may also want to do some informal evaluation, discuss your group guidelines, and decide which study you want to do next. We recommend you visit our website at *SaddlebackResources.com* for more video-based small group studies.

Who is the host?

The host is the person who coordinates and facilitates your group meetings. In addition to a host, we encourage you to select one or more group members to lead your group discussions. Several other responsibilities can be rotated, including refreshments, prayer requests, worship, or keeping up with those who miss a meeting. Shared ownership in the group helps everybody grow.

Where do we find new group members?

Recruiting new members can be a challenge for groups, especially new groups with just a few people, or existing groups that lose a few people along the way. We encourage you to use the Circles of Life diagram on page 97 of this study guide to brainstorm a list of people from your workplace, church, school, neighborhood, family, and so on. Then pray for the people on each member's list. Allow each member to invite several people from their list.

Some groups fear that newcomers will interrupt the intimacy that members have built over time. However, groups that welcome newcomers generally gain strength with the infusion of new blood. Remember, the next person you add just might become a friend for eternity. Logistically, groups find different ways to add members. Some groups remain permanently open, while others choose to open periodically, such as at the beginning or end of a study. If your group becomes too large for easy, face-to-face conversations, you can subgroup, forming a second discussion group in another room.

How do we handle child care needs?

Child care needs must be handled very carefully. This is a sensitive issue. We suggest you seek creative solutions as a group. One common solution is to have the adults meet in the living room and share the cost of a babysitter (or two) who can be with the kids in another part of the house. Another popular option is to have one home for the kids and a second home (close by) for the adults. If desired, the adults could rotate the responsibility of providing a lesson for the kids. This last option is great with school-age kids and can be a huge blessing to families.

What is a spiritual partner?

Spiritual health, like physical health, is often easier to maintain when you are working out with a partner. As you work out what God is working in you, sometimes you need someone to encourage you and help keep you on target. Prayerfully consider which member of your group you might ask to become your spiritual partner. We recommend that men partner with men, women with women, or spouse with spouse. Commit to pray for each other for the duration of this study. Check in throughout the week by phone, or perhaps over coffee, to see what each of you is learning and how you can pray for one another.

How can we encourage group participation?

It is the loving thing to do to let someone else talk. Give people the freedom to speak, but don't insist that they do. Your group will enjoy deeper, more open sharing and discussion if people don't feel pressured to speak up—or if one person doesn't dominate the group's focus.

What if someone is hurting?

For some, love is a difficult subject and this study may bring deep hurts to the surface as people are being healed. Your role as host is to facilitate a loving environment that allows God the opportunity to work in loving ways through group members and through prayer. No one is expected to offer professional counsel. If a difficult relational issue arises beyond the group's ability to support, you may need to privately refer the person to a Christian counselor or pastor.

Small Group Calendar

Healthy groups share responsibilities and group ownership. It might take some time for this to develop. Shared ownership ensures that responsibility for the group doesn't fall to one person. Use the calendar to keep track of social events, mission projects, birthdays, or days off. Complete this calendar at your first or second meeting. Planning ahead will increase attendance and shared ownership.

Date	Lesson	Location	Facilitator	Snack or Meal
10/15	Session One	Chris & Andrea	Steve	Phil & Karen

Group Guidelines

It's a good idea for every group to put words to their shared values, expectations, and commitments. Such guidelines will help you avoid unspoken agendas and unmet expectations. We recommend you discuss your guidelines during Session One in order to lay the foundation for a healthy group experience. Feel free to modify anything that does not work for your group.

We Agree to the Following Values:

Clear Purpose
To grow healthy spiritual lives by building a healthy small group community

Group Attendance
To give priority to the group meeting (call if I am absent or late)

Safe Environment
To create a safe place where people can be heard and feel loved (no quick answers, snap judgments, or simple fixes)

Be Confidential
To keep anything that is shared strictly confidential and within the group

Conflict Resolution
To avoid gossip and to immediately resolve any concerns by following the principles of Matthew 18:15 – 17

Spiritual Health
To give group members permission to speak into my life and help me live a healthy, balanced spiritual life that is pleasing to God

Limit Our Freedom
To limit our freedom by not serving or consuming alcohol during small group meetings or events so as to avoid causing a weaker brother or sister to stumble (1 Corinthians 8:1 – 13; Romans 14:19 – 21)

Welcome Newcomers To invite friends who might benefit from this study and warmly welcome newcomers

Building Relationships To get to know the other members of the group and pray for them regularly

Other   _____

         _____

We Have Also Discussed and Agree on the Following Items:

Child Care   _____

Starting Time _____

Ending Time   _____

If you haven't already done so, take a few minutes to fill out the Small Group Calendar on page 94.

Circles of Life:
Small Group Connections

Discover Who You Can Connect in Community

Use this chart to help carry out one of the values in the Group Guidelines, to "Welcome Newcomers."

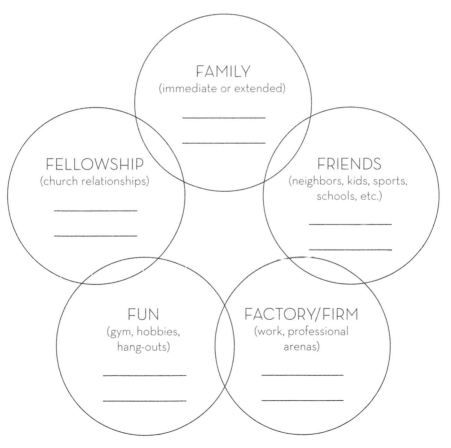

Continued on next page.

Then He said to them, "Follow Me, and I will make you fishers of men." (Matthew 4:19 NKJV)

Follow this simple three-step process:

1. List one to two people in each circle on page 97.

2. Prayerfully select one person or couple from your list and tell your group about them.

3. Give them a call and invite them to your next meeting. Over 50 percent of those invited to a small group say, "Yes!"

Small Group Prayer
and Praise Report

This is a place where you can write each other's requests for prayer.
You can also make a note when God answers a prayer. Pray for
each other's requests. If you're new to group prayer, it's okay to pray
silently or to pray by using just one sentence:

"God, please help _____ to

_____."

Date	Person	Prayer Request	Praise Report

Date	Person	Prayer Request	Praise Report

Small Group Resources

Date	Person	Prayer Request	Praise Report

Date	Person	Prayer Request	Praise Report

Small Group Resources

Releasing Anger
and Bitterness

When we harbor anger and bitterness and refuse to work toward the restoration of broken relationships, we harm others and ourselves as well. We need to prayerfully confront and confess those inner feelings and then surrender them to the loving healing of our heavenly Father. As we do, God will help us to release those unhealthy emotions and to truly forgive others by drawing on his power.

Choose several passages and apply them to your situation. For full impact, you may want to check out other Bible translations for these verses.

1. God calls us to confront our own feelings openly and honestly.

   23Search me, O God, and know my heart; test me and know my anxious thoughts. 24See if there is any offensive way in me, and lead me in the way everlasting. (Psalm 139:23-24 NIV)

   Look after each other so that not one of you will fail to find God's best blessings. Watch out that no bitterness takes root among you, for as it springs up it causes deep trouble, hurting many in their spiritual lives. (Hebrews 12:15 TLB)

   Confess your sins to each other and pray for each other so that you may be healed. The earnest prayer of a righteous person has great power and produces wonderful results. (James 5:16 NLT)

   If we confess our sins, he is faithful and just and will forgive us our sins and purify us from all unrighteousness. (1 John 1:9 NIV)

⁹If anyone claims, "I am living in the light," but hates a Christian brother or sister, that person is still living in darkness. ¹⁰Anyone who loves another brother or sister is living in the light and does not cause others to stumble. ¹¹But anyone who hates another brother or sister is still living and walking in darkness. Such a person does not know the way to go, having been blinded by the darkness. (1 John 2:9-11 NLT)

2. **Our heavenly Father calls us to work actively toward forgiving others and restoring broken relationships.**

If you forgive those who sin against you, your heavenly Father will forgive you. (Matthew 6:14 NLT)

³"Be alert. If you see your friend going wrong, correct him. If he responds, forgive him. ⁴Even if it's personal against you and repeated seven times through the day, and seven times he says, 'I'm sorry, I won't do it again,' forgive him." (Luke 17:3-4 MSG)

¹Follow God's example in everything you do just as a much loved child imitates his father. ²Be full of love for others, following the example of Christ who loved you and gave himself to God as a sacrifice to take away your sins. And God was pleased, for Christ's love for you was like sweet perfume to him. (Ephesians 5:1-2 TLB)

³¹Stop being mean, bad-tempered, and angry. Quarreling, harsh words, and dislike of others should have no place in your lives. ³²Instead, be kind to each other, tenderhearted, forgiving one another, just as God has forgiven you because you belong to Christ. (Ephesians 4:31-32 TLB)

But when you are praying, first forgive anyone you are holding a grudge against, so that your Father in heaven will forgive your sins, too. (Mark 11:25 NLT)

¹³For, dear brothers, you have been given freedom: not freedom to do wrong, but freedom to love and serve each other. ¹⁴For the whole Law can be summed up in this one command: "Love others as you love yourself." ¹⁵But if instead of showing love among yourselves you are always critical and catty, watch out! Beware of ruining each other. (Galatians 5:13 - 15 TLB)

Dear brothers and sisters, if another believer is overcome by some sin, you who are godly should gently and humbly help that person back onto the right path. And be careful not to fall into the same temptation yourself. (Galatians 6:1 NLT)

3. We can depend on God's availability and power.

So let us come boldly to the very throne of God and stay there to receive his mercy and to find grace to help us in our times of need. (Hebrews 4:16 TLB)

Now all glory to God, who is able, through his mighty power at work within us, to accomplish infinitely more than we might ask or think. (Ephesians 3:20 NLT)

And God is able to make all grace abound to you, so that in all things at all times, having all that you need, you will abound in every good work. (2 Corinthians 9:8 NIV)

¹³When you were spiritually dead because of your sins and because you were not free from the power of your sinful self, God made you alive with Christ, and he forgave all our sins. ¹⁴He canceled the debt, which listed all the rules we failed to follow. He took away that record with its rules and nailed it to the cross. ¹⁵God stripped the spiritual rulers and powers of their authority. With the cross, he won the victory and showed the world that they were powerless. (Colossians 2:13 - 15 NCV)

The message about the cross doesn't make any sense to lost people. But for those of us who are being saved, it is God's power at work. (1 Corinthians 1:18 CEV)

Serving
the Lord's Supper

*The Lord Jesus, on the night he was betrayed, took bread, and
when he had given thanks, he broke it and said, "This is my
body, which is for you; do this in remembrance of me." In the
same way, after supper he took the cup, saying, "This cup is
the new covenant in my blood; do this, whenever you drink it, in
remembrance of me." For whenever you eat this bread and drink
this cup, you proclaim the Lord's death until he comes.*
(1 Corinthians 11:23 – 26 NIV)

Steps for Serving Communion

1. Open by sharing about God's love, forgiveness, grace, mercy,
   etc., out of your personal journey. Allow others to share their
   stories.

2. Read the passage: "The Lord Jesus, on the night he was
   betrayed, took bread, and when he had given thanks, he broke
   it and said, 'This is my body, which is for you; do this in
   remembrance of me.'"

3. Pray a short prayer of thanksgiving for the broken body of
   Jesus. Pass the bread around the circle. (This can be a time for
   quiet reflection, singing a simple praise song, or listening to a
   worship CD.)

4. When everyone has been served, remind them that the
   bread represents Jesus' broken body on their behalf. Simply

state: "Jesus said, 'Do this in remembrance of me.' Let's eat together." Then eat the bread as a group.

5. Read the rest of the passage: "In the same way, after supper he took the cup, saying, 'This cup is the new covenant in my blood; do this, whenever you drink it, in remembrance of me.'"

6. Pray a short prayer of thanksgiving for the blood of Jesus. Then pass the cups, either by passing a small tray, serving them individually, or having members pick up a cup from the table.

7. When everyone has been served, remind them the juice represents Christ's blood shed for the forgiveness of their sins. Then simply state: "Take and drink in remembrance of him. Let's drink together."

8. Finish by singing or listening to a simple praise song, or having a time of prayer in thanks to God.

Practical Tips

1. Be sensitive to timing in your meeting.

2. Break up pieces of cracker or bread on a small plate or tray. Don't use large servings of bread or juice. We ask that you only use grape juice, not wine, so you will not cause a group member to struggle.

Communion passages: Matthew 26:26–29; Mark 14:22–25; Luke 22:14–20; 1 Corinthians 10:16–21; 11:17–32

Answer Key

Session One

1. Love is the <u>supreme value</u> in life.
2. Love is the <u>primary objective</u> of life.
    ... nothing I <u>say</u> will matter.
    ... nothing I <u>know</u> will matter.
    ... nothing I <u>believe</u> will matter.
    ... nothing I <u>give</u> will matter.
    ... nothing I <u>accomplish</u> will matter.
3. Love is the <u>greatest power</u> in life.

Session Two

You <u>cooperate</u> with God.
- God's part is to provide the <u>circumstances</u>.
- Your part is to provide the <u>response</u>.
1. Discover a <u>bigger perspective</u>.
2. Deepen <u>your love</u>.
3. Depend on <u>Jesus' power</u>.

Kindness is <u>love in action</u>.
1. Start <u>seeing the needs</u> of people around us.
    Why don't we see the wounds of the people around us? <u>Busyness</u>.
2. <u>Sympathize</u> with people's pain.
3. <u>Seize the moment</u>.
    - You must be willing to be <u>interrupted</u>.
    - You must be willing to <u>take risks</u>.
4. <u>Spend</u> whatever it takes.

Session Three

1. Check your <u>motives</u>.
    What is the right motive? <u>To help, not to hurt</u>.
2. Plan your <u>presentation</u>.
    (1) Plan <u>when</u> you're going to say it.
    (2) Plan <u>what</u> you're going to say.
    (3) Plan <u>how</u> you're going to say it.
    Truth + Tact + Timing = <u>Transformation</u>

3. Give them <u>affirmation</u>.
4. Risk their <u>rejection</u>.

Session Four

1. Forgiveness is not <u>minimizing the seriousness</u> of the offense.
2. Forgiveness is not <u>resuming a relationship</u> without changes.
   - demonstrate <u>genuine repentance</u>.
   - <u>make restitution</u> wherever possible.
   - <u>prove they have changed</u> over time.
1. I relinquish my right <u>to get even</u>.
   - God has <u>forgiven you</u>.
   - Bitterness makes you <u>miserable</u>.
   - You are going to need <u>more forgiveness</u> in the future.
2. I respond to evil <u>with good</u>.
3. I <u>repeat the process</u> as long as necessary.

Session Five

1. Build <u>strong relationships</u>.
2. Give <u>yourself away</u>.
3. Practice <u>self-denial</u>.

Session Six

1. Develop habits that refresh me <u>physically</u>.
   - <u>Rest</u>
   - <u>Balanced diet</u>
   - <u>Regular exercise</u>
2. Develop habits that recharge me <u>emotionally</u>.
   - <u>Solitude</u>
   - <u>Recreation</u>
   - <u>Laughter</u>
3. Develop habits that renew me <u>spiritually</u>.
   - <u>Daily quiet time</u>
   - <u>Small group</u>
   - <u>Worship</u>

Key Verses

I have hidden your word in my heart
that I might not sin against you.
Psalm 119:11 (NIV)

One of the most effective ways to drive deeply into our lives
the principles we are learning in this series is to memorize key
Scriptures. For many, memorization is a new concept or one that has
been difficult in the past. We encourage you to stretch yourself and
try to memorize these six key verses. If possible, memorize these as
a group and make them part of your group time. You may cut these
apart and carry them in your wallet.

SESSION ONE	SESSION TWO
Let love be your highest goal!	*Love is patient, love is kind.*
1 Corinthians 14:1 (NLT)	1 Corinthians 13:4 (NIV)
SESSION THREE	SESSION FOUR
Love … rejoices with the truth.	*Love … doesn't keep a record*
1 Corinthians 13:6 (NIV)	*of the wrongs of others.*
	1 Corinthians 13:5 (CEV)
SESSION FIVE	SESSION SIX
Love isn't selfish.	*[Love] always protects, always trusts,*
1 Corinthians 13:5 (CEV)	*always hopes, always perseveres.*
	1 Corinthians 13:7 (NIV)

Share Your Thoughts

With the Author: Your comments will be forwarded to the author when you send them to *zauthor@zondervan.com.*

With Zondervan: Submit your review of this book by writing to *zreview@zondervan.com.*

Free Online Resources at
www.zondervan.com

Zondervan AuthorTracker: Be notified whenever your favorite authors publish new books, go on tour, or post an update about what's happening in their lives at www.zondervan.com/authortracker.

Daily Bible Verses and Devotions: Enrich your life with daily Bible verses or devotions that help you start every morning focused on God. Visit www.zondervan.com/newsletters.

Free Email Publications: Sign up for newsletters on Christian living, academic resources, church ministry, fiction, children's resources, and more. Visit www.zondervan.com/newsletters.

Zondervan Bible Search: Find and compare Bible passages in a variety of translations at www.zondervanbiblesearch.com.

Other Benefits: Register yourself to receive online benefits like coupons and special offers, or to participate in research.

ZONDERVAN®

ZONDERVAN.com/
AUTHOR**TRACKER**
follow your favorite authors